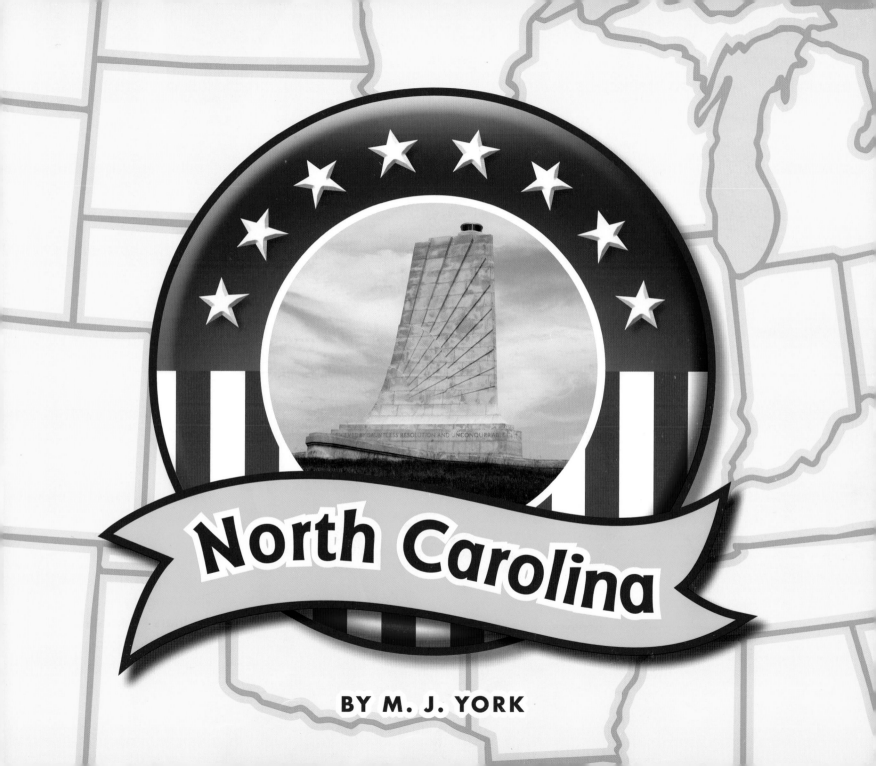

North Carolina

BY M. J. YORK

Published by The Child's World®
1980 Lookout Drive • Mankato, MN 56003-1705
800-599-READ • www.childsworld.com

ACKNOWLEDGMENTS
The Child's World®: Mary Berendes, Publishing Director
The Design Lab: Design and production
Red Line Editorial: Editorial direction

PHOTO CREDITS: T. Markley/Shutterstock Images, cover, 1, 3; Matt Kania/
Map Hero, Inc., 4, 5; Denis Tangney Jr./iStockphoto, 7; Matej Krajcovic/
iStockphoto, 9; iStockphoto, 10; Matt Smith/iStockphoto, 11; Steve Humbert/
AP Images, 13; Photolibrary, 15; Shutterstock Images, 17; Tom Strattman/AP
Images, 19; William Britten/iStockphoto, 21; One Mile Up, 22; Quarter-dollar
coin image from the United States Mint, 22

LIBRARY OF CONGRESS CATALOGING-IN-PUBLICATION DATA
York, M. J., 1983–
  North Carolina / by M.J. York.
     p. cm.
  Includes bibliographical references and index.
  ISBN 978-1-60253-477-3 (library bound : alk. paper)
  1. North Carolina—Juvenile literature. I. Title.

F254.3.Y67 2010
975.6—dc22

                                        2010019196

Printed in the United States of America in Mankato, Minnesota.
July 2010
F11538

On the cover:
The Wright
Brothers National
Memorial is in
North Carolina.

CONTENTS

4 Geography

6 Cities

8 Land

10 Plants and Animals

12 People and Work

14 History

16 Ways of Life

18 Famous People

20 Famous Places

22 *State Symbols*

23 *Glossary*

24 *Further Information*

24 *Index*

Geography

Let's explore North Carolina! North Carolina is in the southeast United States. The Atlantic Ocean is to the east.

WEST VIRGINIA

KENTUCKY

VIRGINIA

TENNESSEE

Winston-Salem • Greensboro

Blue Ridge
Mountains

Great Smoky
Mountains

Great Smoky
Mountains
National Park

High Point
Lexington •

Durham
Chapel Hill •

★ Raleigh

NORTH CAROLINA

Charlotte • • Concord

• Smithfield

• Fayetteville

Kitty
Hawk

Roanoke
Island

Cape
Hatteras

• Beaufort

SOUTH CAROLINA

GEORGIA

Atlantic
Ocean

NORTH
WEST   EAST
SOUTH

5

Cities

Raleigh is the capital of North Carolina. Charlotte is the largest city in the state. Nearly 700,000 people live there. Durham and Greensboro are other well-known cities.

Raleigh is named after English explorer Sir Walter Raleigh. ▶

Land

North Carolina is sandy and **swampy** near the ocean. The land rises gently in the west. It rises up into the Great Smoky Mountains and the Blue Ridge Mountains.

The Great Smoky Mountains are often covered with a fog that looks like smoke. ▶

Plants and Animals

The state tree of North Carolina is the pine tree. The state bird is the cardinal. The male is bright red. The state **mammal** is the gray squirrel.

Many types of pine trees grow in North Carolina. ▶

North Carolina has two state berries. They are the blueberry and the strawberry.

People and Work

More than 9 million people live in North Carolina. Farming is very important here. Hogs, chickens, and tobacco are important North Carolina goods. Fabric and furniture are made in North Carolina. Many people are part of the **military**. Many people work in factories. Others work in **research** and banking.

North Carolina has rich soil that is good for farming. ▶

History

People from England tried to settle on Roanoke Island in the 1500s. The **colony** was off the coast of what is now North Carolina. But the colony was soon deserted. New settlers came in the 1600s. North Carolina was one of the 13 original colonies. It became the twelfth state on November 21, 1789. During the U.S. **Civil War**, the state left the United States to join the **Confederate States of America**. North Carolina rejoined the United States in 1868.

This gravestone stands for the deserted colony on Roanoke Island. ▶

ON THIS SITE IN JULY-AUGUST, 1585
O S COLONISTS SENT OUT FROM ENGLAND
BY SIR WALTER RALEIGH BUILT A FORT CALL
ED BY THEM
THE NEW FORT IN VIRGINIA
THESE COLONISTS WERE THE FIRST SET-
TLERS OF THE ENGLISH RACE IN AMERICA.
THEY RETURNED TO ENGLAND IN JULY 1586.
WITH SIR FRANCIS DRAKE
NEAR THIS PLACE WAS BORN ON THE 18
OF AUGUST 1587.
VIRGINIA DARE
THE FIRST CHILD OF ENGLISH PARENTS BORN
IN AMERICA-DAUGHTER OF ANANIAS DARE
ELEANOR WHITE WHO WERE MEMBERS OF
ANOTHER BAND OF COLONISTS SENT OUT BY
SIR WALTER RALEIGH IN 1587.
ON SUNDAY AUGUST 20 1587 V
GINIA DARE WAS BAPTIZED MANTEO
THE FRIENDLY CHIEF OF THE HATTERAS
WAS BAPTIZED ON THE SUN
CEL THESE BAPTISMS ARE THE
KNOWN CELEBRATIONS OF CHRIST
RAMENT IN THE TERRITORY OF THE
TEEN ORIGINAL UNITED STATES

The Wright brothers flew the first airplane near Kitty Hawk, North Carolina, in 1903.

Ways of Life

People enjoy North Carolina's many golf courses. Visitors like to fish, swim at the beaches, and boat, too. Many people in North Carolina enjoy eating **barbecue**.

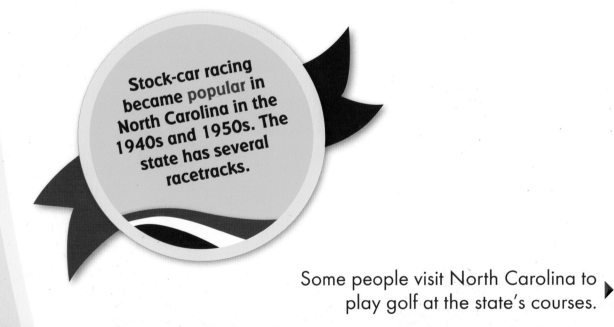

Stock-car racing became popular in North Carolina in the 1940s and 1950s. The state has several racetracks.

Some people visit North Carolina to play golf at the state's courses. ▶

Famous People

Author O. Henry was born in North Carolina. Poets Maya Angelou and Carl Sandburg lived in North Carolina later in their lives. Car racers Dale Earnhardt Jr. and Richard Petty are also from the state.

Virginia Dare was the first English child born in America. She was born on Roanoke Island in 1587.

Dale Earnhardt Jr.'s father and grandfather were also race-car drivers. ▶

Famous Places

For many years, the Cape Hatteras **lighthouse** protected ships from the rocky coast. It is the tallest lighthouse in the United States. To the west lies the Great Smoky Mountains National Park. A part of the Appalachian Trail also runs through North Carolina.

The Cape Hatteras lighthouse is in the Outer Banks, ▶
a popular place to visit in North Carolina.

State Symbols

Seal

The state seal of North Carolina has two women on it. The women stand for liberty and plenty. Go to childsworld.com/links for a link to North Carolina's state Web site, where you can get a firsthand look at the state seal.

Flag

The state flag has red, white, and blue stripes and a white star.

Quarter

The North Carolina state quarter has an airplane to stand for the Wright Brothers' first flight. The quarter came out in 2001.

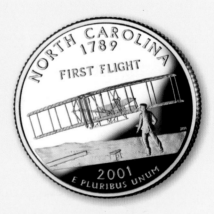

Glossary

barbecue (BAR-buh-kyoo): Barbecue is grilled meat. Barbecue is popular in North Carolina.

Civil War (SIV-il WOR): In the United States, the Civil War was a war fought between the Northern and the Southern states from 1861 to 1865. North Carolina was part of the Confederate States of America during the Civil War.

colony (KOL-uh-nee): A colony is an area of land that is newly settled and is controlled by a government of another land. North Carolina was an English colony.

Confederate States of America (kun-FED-ur-ut STAYTS UHV uh-MAYR-uh-kuh): The Confederate States of America was the group of 11 states that left the United States to form their own nation during the U.S. Civil War. North Carolina was part of the Confederate States of America.

lighthouse (LYT-howss): A lighthouse is a tall building near an ocean or large lake that uses lights to warn ships of danger. The tallest lighthouse in the United States is in North Carolina.

mammal (MAM-ul): A mammal is a warm-blooded animal that has a backbone and hair; female mammals can produce milk to feed their babies. North Carolina's state mammal is the gray squirrel.

memorial (muh-MOR-ee-ul): A memorial is a place or thing that honors people or events. The Wright Brothers National Memorial is in North Carolina.

military (MIL-uh-tayr-ee): The military is the armed forces of a country. Many people in North Carolina are part of the military.

popular (POP-yuh-lur): To be popular is to be enjoyed by many people. Stock-car racing is popular in North Carolina.

research (REE-surch): Research is studying or experimenting on something. Some people in North Carolina work on scientific research.

seal (SEEL): A seal is a symbol a state uses for government business. North Carolina's state seal shows two women who stand for liberty and plenty.

swampy (SWAHMP-ee): If land is swampy, it has plants and is covered in water. North Carolina's eastern coast is sandy and swampy.

symbols (SIM-bulz): Symbols are pictures or things that stand for something else. Symbols for the state are on North Carolina's seal.

Further Information

Books

Crane, Carol. *T is for Tar Heel: A North Carolina Alphabet.* Chelsea, MI: Sleeping Bear Press, 2003.

Crane, Carol. *Wright Numbers: A North Carolina Number Book.* Chelsea, MI: Sleeping Bear Press, 2005.

Keller, Laurie. *The Scrambled States of America.* New York: Henry Holt, 2002.

Web Sites

Visit our Web site for links about North Carolina: *childsworld.com/links*

Note to Parents, Teachers, and Librarians: We routinely verify our Web links to make sure they are safe and active sites. So encourage your readers to check them out!

Index

activities, 16
Appalachian Trail, 20
Atlantic Ocean, 4, 8

Blue Ridge Mountains, 8

Cape Hatteras
  lighthouse, 20
capital, 6

Great Smoky Mountains, 8, 20

jobs, 12

population, 12

state berries, 11
state bird, 10
state mammal, 10

state tree, 10

tourism, 16

U.S. Civil War, 14